WOULD YOU RATHER...?

The Naughty Conversation Game for Couples

HOT AND SEXY EDITION

J.R. James

D1372338

Spice up your love life even more, and explore all the discussion books for couples by J.R. James:

Love and Relationship Books for Couples

Would You Rather...? The Romantic Conversation Game for Couples (Love and Romance Edition)

Sexy Game Books for Couples

Would You Rather...? The Naughty Conversation Game for Couples (Hot and Sexy Edition)

Truth or Dare? The Sexy Game of Naughty Choices (Hot and Wild Edition)

Never Have I Ever... An Exciting and Sexy Game for Adults (Hot and Dirty Edition)

The Hot or Not Quiz for Couples: The Sexy Game of Naughty Questions and Revealing Answers

Sexy Discussion Books for Couples

Let's Talk Sexy: Essential Conversation Starters to Explore Your Lover's Secret Desires and Transform Your Sex Life

All **THREE** *Let's Talk About...* sexy question books in one massive volume for one low price. Save now!

Let's Talk About... Sexual Fantasies and Desires: Questions and Conversation Starters for Couples Exploring Their Sexual Interests

Let's Talk About... Non-Monogamy: Questions and Conversation Starters for Couples Exploring Open Relationships, Swinging, or Polyamory

Let's Talk About... Kinks and Fetishes: Questions and Conversation Starters for Couples Exploring Their Sexual Wild Side

Sign up for our mailing list and be entered to win a FREE copy of any of the sexy question books by J.R. James. New winner selected every month!

Sign up here:

https://mailchi.mp/a75ed05fd334/jrjames

HOW TO PLAY THE GAME

The rules for this game are very simple:

There needs to be at least two people to play. (It's a great game for couples!) If you and your partner are really adventurous, try playing with another couple, or even more people at a party. The more people, the more fun!

Each page has a hypothetical question that begins with "Would you rather...?" and ends with two choices. Take turns asking and answering the questions. **You must choose one of the options, and no skipping the questions.**

As you spend time discussing the answers, you'll soon you'll find yourselves smiling, laughing, and enjoying the sexually charged conversation. Who knows? You may even discover new sexual possibilities for your relationship. Just have fun! It's the game where everyone wins!

Enjoy!

1
Would you rather…

Watch your partner have a hot and heavy make out session with someone you don't know,

OR

Listen to them have loud, wild sex behind closed doors with someone you do know?

2

Would you rather…

Never have another orgasm for the rest of your life,

OR

Have a perpetual orgasm that never stops?

3

Would you rather…

Try something new and kinky in bed,

OR

Have "typical", but very passionate sex?

<u>4</u>
Would you rather…

Have orgasms that last
three times longer than
normal,

OR

Have sex three times more
often than you typically
do?

5

Would you rather…

Go to work or school completely naked for one day,

OR

Be naked every time you're in the car for the next year?

<u>6</u>

Would you rather…

Be a terrible kisser,

OR

Be awful at oral sex?

<u>7</u>

Would you rather…

Accidentally send nude photos to your ex,

OR

Accidentally send them to a neighbor?

<u>8</u>

Would you rather…

Have public sex in a nearly empty sports stadium during a game,

OR

Have sex in a darkened, but crowded, movie theater?

<u>9</u>
Would you rather…

Have your lover kiss every square inch of your body,

OR

Have your lover lick you from head to toe?

_10_

Would you rather…

Make out with your boss,

OR

Watch your partner make out with their boss?

<u>11</u>

Would you rather…

Have sex with a biter,

OR

Have sex with a screamer?

_12_

Would you rather…

Be a porn star,

OR

Date a porn star?

13

Would you rather...

Mistakenly send a dirty text message to your boss,

OR

Mistakenly send a dirty text message to your mom?

<u>14</u>
Would you rather…

Be really good at foreplay
and bad at sex,

OR

Be really good at sex and
terrible at foreplay?

15

Would you rather…

Have sex with only one person all your life,

OR

Always have sex in the same position?

_**16**_

Would you rather...

Wear nipple clamps for an entire day,

OR

Have a small dildo in your ass for the day?

_17_
Would you rather…

Have a lover who never stops talking during sex,

OR

Have one that never makes a sound?

_18_

Would you rather…

Watch your ex having sex,

OR

Have your ex watch you having sex?

_**19**_
Would you rather…

Masturbate in front of a crowd,

OR

Watch a crowd of people masturbate in front of you?

_20_

Would you rather…

Use chocolate syrup during sex,

OR

Use whipped cream?

21

Would you rather…

Have a lover who is slow, gentle, and can last for hours,

OR

Have a lover who's passionate and energetic, but can only last a few minutes?

22
Would you rather...

Cry every time you orgasmed,

OR

Laugh uncontrollably?

23

Would you rather…

Sleep with the first person who hits on you in a bar,

OR

Sleep with the first person who hits on you at a bookstore?

<u>24</u>

Would you rather…

Take a lover with terrible body odor,

OR

One with horribly bad breath?

<u>25</u>

Would you rather…

Have a partner who can never lie (even if the truth is painful to hear),

OR

Be with a partner who always says what you want to hear (even if it's not true)?

_26_

Would you rather…

Give a golden shower,

OR

Receive one?

27

Would you rather…

Have a lover who can never orgasm,

OR

One that can never make you orgasm?

_**28**_

Would you rather…

Date someone with a perfect body, but who's boring in bed,

OR

Date someone who's amazing in bed, but who looks average?

29

Would you rather…

Give up masturbating for a year,

OR

Give up sex for 4 months?

_**30**_

Would you rather…

Be with a lover who has no hair anywhere on their head or body,

OR

Have one who is excessively hairy everywhere?

_31_

Would you rather…

Your partner found oral
sex disgusting,

OR

Was constantly obsessed
with anal sex?

_32_

Would you rather...

Sleep with the movie or music star of your choice,

OR

Have sex with any sports star or athlete?

_33_

Would you rather…

Be with a lover who would try anything you could ever want in bed, but is bad at sex,

OR

Have a lover who is great at sex, but extremely limited in what they would do?

<u>34</u>
Would you rather...

Have sex with your partner all day long,

OR

Have sex with your partner all night long?

_35_

Would you rather…

Give a handjob to your partner in public,

OR

Receive a handjob from your lover in public?

36

Would you rather…

Work at a strip club,

OR

Have a partner who works at a strip club?

<u>37</u>
Would you rather…

Give a lap dance to one of your parents,

OR

Get a lap dance from one of your parents?

38

Would you rather…

Accidentally scream the wrong name in bed,

OR

Hear your partner scream the wrong name in bed?

<u>39</u>

Would you rather…

Have your toes sucked during sex,

OR

Have your fingers sucked during sex?

<u>40</u>

Would you rather…

Be with a lover who was incredibly romantic,

OR

Have a lover who was super kinky?

<u>41</u>

Would you rather…

Be told you were terrible at kissing,

OR

Be told you were awful at oral sex?

<u>42</u>

Would you rather…

Have sex in bright lighting,

OR

Have sex in complete darkness?

_43_

Would you rather…

Sleep with your high school crush,

OR

Your celebrity crush?

<u>44</u>

Would you rather…

Let your significant other sleep with your best friend,

OR

Let them sleep with your worst enemy?

_45_

Would you rather…

Watch something erotic with your lover,

OR

Listen to your lover read erotica while you touch yourself?

46

Would you rather…

Have a threesome,

OR

Participate in an orgy?

_47_

Would you rather…

Pay for sex,

OR

Get paid for it?

$\underline{48}$

Would you rather…

Watch a girl on girl video,

OR

Watch a guy on guy?

_49_

Would you rather…

Only be able to have sex in cars,

OR

Only be able to have sex in the shower?

<u>50</u>

Would you rather…

Never be able to masturbate again,

OR

Never be able to eat solid foods again?

_51_

Would you rather…

Have an obvious orgasm every time you or someone else says your name,

OR

Orgasm every time you're near a piece of fruit?

52

Would you rather…

Have a sexual fling with someone ten years older than yourself,

OR

Have one with someone ten years younger?

53

Would you rather…

Date someone much, much more attractive than you,

OR

Date someone slightly less attractive?

<u>54</u>

Would you rather…

Your partner insist on wearing an animal costume during sex,

OR

Have them insist on you wearing the costume?

55

Would you rather…

Go out for a wild night on the town,

OR

Have a cozy, intimate evening at home?

56

Would you rather…

Be with a partner who was excessively affectionate in public,

OR

Who never showed affection in public?

57

Would you rather...

Fall asleep with your lover,

OR

Wake up next to them?

58

Would you rather…

Have sex on live television,

OR

Never have sex ever again?

59

Would you rather...

Have your lover be more
dominant in bed,

OR

Have your lover be more
submissive?

_60_

Would you rather…

Watch a porno starring all of your co-workers,

OR

Or all of your partner's exes?

_**61**_

Would you rather…

Watch your partner
masturbate,

OR

Have your partner watch
you masturbate?

62

Would you rather…

Watch your significant other have sex with their best friend,

OR

Watch them have sex with your best friend?

<u>63</u>

Would you rather…

Have more foreplay in
your life,

OR

Have more sex?

64

Would you rather...

Give up kissing for the rest of your life,

OR

Give up any foreplay?

65

Would you rather…

Be with a lover who's abnormally tall,

OR

Incredibly short?

66

Would you rather…

Find out your lover had sex with their ex,

OR

Find out they had sex with their distant cousin?

<u>67</u>
Would you rather…

Only have rough sex for the rest of your life,

OR

Have only gentle sex all the time?

_68_

Would you rather…

Talk dirty to your lover while they're trying to work,

OR

Listen to them talk dirty to you while you're trying to work?

69

Would you rather…

Have sex in a hot tub with another couple,

OR

Have sex in a pool with lots of people around?

70

Would you rather…

Go to work with your neck covered in hickeys,

OR

Go to a family celebration covered in them?

71

Would you rather…

Publicly ask ten people you don't know if they'd let *you* give them oral sex,

OR

Ask three co-workers or neighbors if *they* would give you oral sex?

72

Would you rather...

Have sex in the middle of the woods,

OR

On a sandy beach?

<u>73</u>

Would you rather…

Be teased with ice cubes during foreplay,

OR

Teased with warm wax dripped on your skin?

<u>74</u>

Would you rather…

Have a long session of phone sex with a lover,

OR

Have your lover send you sexy texts throughout the day?

75

Would you rather…

Have sex while in a moving car,

OR

Have sex in a plane's bathroom?

<u>76</u>
Would you rather…

Have it come out that your significant other was a former porn star,

OR

Have it become public that your mother was an adult actress?

77

Would you rather…

Be with someone who loves to striptease,

OR

Who is talented at teasing you with their tongue?

_78_

Would you rather…

Receive a massage from a stranger that leads to sex,

OR

Give an "innocent" massage to a friend that ends up leading to sex?

79

Would you rather…

Date someone who has a brilliant mind,

OR

Date someone that has a hilarious personality?

_80_

Would you rather…

Find out your significant other slept with your parent in the past,

OR

Find out your ex now sleeps with your parent?

81

Would you rather…

Only be able to kiss with your eyes open,

OR

Only be able to have sex with your eyes closed?

_82_

Would you rather…

Be teased while
blindfolded,

OR

Handcuffed to your bed?

<u>*83*</u>

Would you rather…

Your first sexual experience be with another virgin,

OR

Someone who has had many sexual experiences and multiple partners?

<u>84</u>

Would you rather…

Have a leaked video of you masturbating,

OR

A video of you having sex?

_85_

Would you rather…

Be gagged and blindfolded during sex,

OR

Blindfold and gag your lover?

<u>86</u>

Would you rather...

Have a drunken one night stand with someone much older than yourself,

OR

Much younger?

_87_

Would you rather…

Get a large penis tattooed
on your chest,

OR

Have a large vagina
tattooed on your back?

88

Would you rather…

Have extremely hot, but quiet, sex in a library,

OR

Or an erotic sexual fling in a museum?

89

Would you rather...

Call your lover filthy
names during sex,

OR

Have them talk dirty to
you while having sex?

90

Would you rather…

Roleplay with your significant other while you're both dressed as superheroes,

OR

You both roleplay in costumes as animated characters?

91

Would you rather…

Be a sex slave for a month,

OR

Wear a chastity device for a month?

<u>92</u>

Would you rather...

Have a threesome with your partner and a third person you know,

OR

Be the "third" with a couple you don't know?

93
Would you rather…

Let your significant other have sex with one of your friends,

OR

With one of *their* friends?

_94_

Would you rather…

Not be able to see during sex,

OR

Not be able to touch?

<u>95</u>

Would you rather…

Only have sex with the first person you slept with,

OR

Only ever have sex with the last person you slept with?

96

Would you rather…

Have a lover covered in tattoos,

OR

One with piercings all over their body?

<u>97</u>

Would you rather…

Have a partner who doesn't love you, but is very sexually attracted to you,

OR

A partner who is physically repulsed by you, but loves you dearly?

_98_

Would you rather…

Experience orgasms randomly all day long,

OR

Never masturbate again?

99
Would you rather…

Have your partner fall asleep every time the two of you are having sex ,

OR

Will only agree to sex between the hours of 9 a.m. to 3 p.m.?

100

Would you rather…

Only be able to have sex at work for the rest of your life,

OR

Or only ever be able to have sex outside?

_101_

Would you rather...

Cuddle with a one night stand,

OR

Have them leave as soon as possible?

_102_

Would you rather…

Have a foursome with your partner and another couple,

OR

Swap partners with the couple and have sex in separate rooms?

103

Would you rather…

Find out your partner is secretly a stripper,

OR

Find out they're a high-priced prostitute?

<u>104</u>

Would you rather…

Feel horny all the time, but never have sex,

OR

Never feel aroused, but be able to have sex whenever you'd like?

105

Would you rather…

Laugh uncontrollably during sex,

OR

Cry inconsolably during foreplay?

_106_

Would you rather…

Loudly announce your dirtiest sexual fantasies in front of your co-workers,

OR

In front of your family reunion?

_107_

Would you rather…

Always have sex before breakfast,

OR

Only have sex after dinner?

_108_

Would you rather…

Have sex outside in the middle of a hurricane,

OR

In a blizzard?

109

Would you rather…

Make out with a person wearing clown makeup,

OR

A person who is dressed in a realistic zombie costume?

_110_

Would you rather…

Be able to make yourself orgasm any time you like,

OR

Be able to make anyone else orgasm at will?

Spice up your love life even more, and explore all the discussion books for couples by J.R. James:

Love and Relationship Books for Couples

Would You Rather...? The Romantic Conversation Game for Couples (Love and Romance Edition)

Sexy Game Books for Couples

Would You Rather...? The Naughty Conversation Game for Couples (Hot and Sexy Edition)

Truth or Dare? The Sexy Game of Naughty Choices (Hot and Wild Edition)

Never Have I Ever... An Exciting and Sexy Game for Adults (Hot and Dirty Edition)

The Hot or Not Quiz for Couples: The Sexy Game of Naughty Questions and Revealing Answers

Sexy Discussion Books for Couples

Let's Talk Sexy: Essential Conversation Starters to Explore Your Lover's Secret Desires and Transform Your Sex Life

All **THREE** *Let's Talk About...* sexy question books in one massive volume for one low price. Save now!

Let's Talk About... Sexual Fantasies and Desires: Questions and Conversation Starters for Couples Exploring Their Sexual Interests

Let's Talk About... Non-Monogamy: Questions and Conversation Starters for Couples Exploring Open Relationships, Swinging, or Polyamory

Let's Talk About... Kinks and Fetishes: Questions and Conversation Starters for Couples Exploring Their Sexual Wild Side

Sign up for our mailing list and be entered to win a FREE copy of any of the sexy question books by J.R. James. New winner selected every month!

Sign up here:

https://mailchi.mp/a75ed05fd334/jrjames

ABOUT THE AUTHOR

J.R. James is a best-selling author who has a passion for bringing couples closer together and recharging their sexual intimacy. Erotic discussion is a powerfully sexy thing, and his conversation starter books have helped many couples reach new and sexually exciting heights in their relationships!

Sexy conversation with your partner is a magical, bonding experience. Through these best-selling question books, couples can find an easy way to engage in open and honest sexual discussion with each other. The result is a relationship that is both erotically charged and sexually liberating.

Made in the USA
Middletown, DE
06 August 2020